PERSPECTIVE REFLECTIONS
in RHYME

Rhyme · Sonnets · Prose · Haiku · Limericks

David Watson

enjoy!

Mike Henry **TKACHUK**

Tellwell Talent
www.tellwell.ca

ISBN
978-1-77370-770-9 (Hardcover)
978-1-77370-769-3 (Paperback)

I dedicate this book to my wife Dolores
Who stood by me and encouraged me to
pursue my passion for poetry writing.
I am grateful to her for her
patience and understanding
During this my second volume of poetry

Rhyme

Our Heritage

When our ancestors left their beloved Ukraine
One hundred and twenty-five years ago,
In tears they abandoned their native land
To forge a niche on a democratic plain
Where the buffalo roam and maples grow.

So, they sailed across the ocean wide
Bringing forth saws, picks, and axes
With a sheer desire and keen resolve
To clear the land and craft their homes;
Hard work was their natural praxis.

With long delays in immigration queues
Diseases struck from malnutrition.
Children and seniors most afflicted
Succumbed to their ailments on the way.
Impeding the pioneers' costly mission.

These hardships did not crush their dreams
To establish a homestead on the prairies;
Regrettably the land they chose in haste
Was swampy, sandy or rife with stones,
 More suitable for sheep and dairies.

But, these settlers were agriculturalists
Weaned from good European stock
Well-homed in prodigious farming skills.
Through thrift and toil, by the grace of God
They carved their destiny out of pure bedrock.

Our Heritage *(CONTINUED)*

When conflict broke in thirty-nine
A call to battle was the resounding plea.
The able donned their combat boots,
Shouldered arms, and went to war
To keep this county safe and free.

As families grew and farmers prospered
Choice careers would soon abound.
With mastery of the vernacular,
Through education and tenacity
Professional paths were easily ground.

In federal, provincial and municipal realms
Where progenies assume executive roles
They vow to keep this country great
With democracy as the bonding glue
And faith in God to appease the souls.

We reminisce about our beleaguered past,
Then respectfully put it all behind.
For it's the glowing future we now embrace
And the daunting task that lies ahead
For generations to build in kind.

Ukrainian blood flows through our veins
A proud vestige of our Slavic race
But Canada is our land of birth,
Where hopes, dreams and lives now flourish
That bears our final resting place!

Gift of Love

As you kneel at the foot of the crèche
On blessed Christmas morn,
Note the humble and lowly milieu
Of the barn where Jesus was born.

Mary and Joseph stand watching
O'er their darling and lovely boy child;
While Magi and shepherds look on
At the baby, so meek and so mild.

It must boggle one's erudite mind,
How a virgin gave birth to a child,
Or, why God sent His Own Son
To die on the cross undefiled.

His love for humanity was boundless
As He offered His Son to the world,
In belief they would receive Him,
But, an alter scenario unfurled.

For some of His children dissented,
Freely drifting away from the fold.
Rejecting His love and protection;
Betrayed for thirty pieces and sold.

Let all of one mind at Christmas,
Extend a sincere loving hand
To our families, our neighbors and friends,
And bring Christ back to this secular land.

A Single Red Rose

From a nosegay of sweet-scented roses
A-bloom in the garden of rhyme,
I plucked the loveliest one of them all,
To offer my sweet Valentine!

A single red rose on slender green stem
Mid foliage, a-glistening with dew —
A symbol of love so yearning within,
For someone as precious as you!

This blossom imbued with fragrant perfume
With petals so fragile and fair,
Comes with a heart I offer to you;
Please handle with ardor and care!

Should you discover the gift I impart
Does one day just whither and flake,
Yet my love will endure the test of time,
This promise I solemnly make!

If Only

His work was over for the day
His homeward drive an hour away.
Visions flashed through his pondering mind
Of evening pleasures, he would find;
The friends he'd meet at the gym,
And thoughts of looking sleek and trim.

When he reached his parent's gate
The nosh was steaming on the plate.
Quickly stuffing his hungry mouth
He grabbed his bag and darted out.
When mother heard the engine roar
Her good-bye omened forever more.

Down the gravel road he raced.
In a cloud of dust, he left his place.
In such a rush to be somewhere,
He jumped the crossroad unaware
That a car was streaming from the west;
The horrendous crash laid him to rest.

A young man's life was spent that day,
And all his schooling thrown away.
A mother's tears dropped like rain,
A father's heart broke in twain,
A fiancée's dreams died that eve,
A brother's friendship took its leave.

Constant "ifs" run through their minds:
If only he had lingered behind!
If only he had looked both ways!
If only he stayed home that day!
If only we could turn back time,
Everything would be just fine!

Prayers and pleading are for naught
When tragic action has been wrought.
When laws of nature have been broken
Tragedy is the gravest token.
As on life's highway in travelling mode,
Stay alert and mind the road.

A Golden Jubilee

Dauntless in their quest for righteousness,
Fledgling lovebirds chaste and priss,
Resolved to curb their autonomy;
Supplanting it with connubial bliss.

The bride, in gown of snowy white
The groom attired in ebony
Stood before God's Holy Altar
Exchanging vows of fidelity.

Fleeting years spawned countless changes
Auburn hair turned silver gray.
Their progeny grown self-reliant
Long renounced their refuge stay.

Trials and burdens they surmounted
Attests to life so loyally played;
Their lives inscribed in gilded toner,
Extolled on parchments worn and frayed.

Replicating that familiar presence
Fifty years now in review
Two gentle hearts in perfect rhythm
Their marriage vows come to renew.

They petition God for His blessing
To support their spousal role
'til heaven beckons them up yonder
To their merited eternal goal.

A Tribute to Mothers

Wishing you songbirds
To welcome your day.
Wishing you flowers
To brighten your way.
Wishing you laughter
To abridge your strife.
Wishing you joy
To lighten your life.

Preparing your breakfast
In a special way.
Buying you chocolates
To sweeten your day.
Washing the dishes
So you may rest.
But saying "Thank you"
Is by far the best!

A Woodland Hideaway

There is a land far removed from urban life
To which I waft across the miles with blissful gain.
 Where to naught diminish worldly shams and strife
From a careworn mind cluttered with city bane.

In those enchanted woodland hideaways
Undaunted squirrels frolic freely about the land.
Where neighbors dwell in filial ways
Ever ready to extend a helping hand.

The towering oaks wave fond good-byes
To the gypsy clouds seeking a lasting home.
The lure of the whispering pines' audible sighs
Disturbed by whistling elk on the roam.

The falling dusk bids the sun to hide
And Monet brushes the sky with a silver moon,
I bathe in the stillness of eventide
And the haunting call of the lonesome loon.

The peacefulness these woodlands yield
Is like a tranquil symphony of rhyme;
A fundamental structure of the natural field
Akin to Newtonian time.

Home Invasion

In the wee hours of that sinister morn
A shady prowler came skulking by
In search of a treasure to purloin;
The gang's initiation rites to ply.

He planted his hoof with such violent force
On the sturdy metal-cladded door,
That it tore the portal off its pins,
Hurling it crashing to the floor.

The horrendous din by that felonious act
Shattered the calm that frightful night,
And roused the couple with a start
From the restful arms of Morpheus' might.

It brought to the fore a hideous boil –
A vestige of iniquity on the take
Straight from the gaping maw of Hell
That harbored this slimy, slithery snake.

Although a new door fills the gaping hole
With the costly repairs, now complete,
Nothing could heal and restore to ideal
The fragile psyche so shaken and deplete.

Henceforth every creak and thump in the night
Replays images of that unsettling morn
When a single moment of terror shaped
A lasting garment of angst to scorn.

The Highway of Heroes

Along a short stretch of highway
On the eminent Four – 0 – One,
Winds a cavalcade of black limos
Bearing a fallen daughter or son.

On this sad and solemn journey,
Heart-wrenching and wrought with tears,
Countless kindred souls stand waiting
For a glimpse of the fallen warriors.

To our blessed protectors of freedom,
And the costly price they had paid,
Mere strangers reach out to pay tribute
For the sacrifice, our heroes have made

Emotions run high for the parents,
Their sad hearts in sobs displayed;
Commingled with pride and honour
For the forfeit, their progenies made.

May their sacrifice long be remembered;
Their names forever etched in stone,
As they make their last pitch for freedom
On this Highway, leading them home.

Hope Beyond Hopelessness

The Bomber's arena stood silently still
As the game drew to half time.
The scoreboard favoured the visiting Greens
By a spread of twenty-eight nil.

The Blues attempted time and again
To outscore their formidable foe.
Adamant were they to appease their fans
With a long awaited overdue, win.

But, the harder they tried to evoke some cheers
From their now disillusioned fans,
The more errors they made with each play,
Arousing just scorn and jeers.

A chance for a score was fading
As the carrot kept moving beyond reach.
Fumbles and errors kept plaguing the game
With each successive attempt, they made.

An irksome realization soon arose
Failing their desperate attempts to score,
A sound defeat would be their lot
When the fourth quarter drew to a close.

Achieving their goal, came to a stop.
As the brass ring shifted beyond their reach.
But, recalling the legend of Pandora 's Box
They vowed to never give up!

Despite their dismal crushing toss
It did not stifle their metal resolve.
To fight on and win future games
Notwithstanding their fifty-two loss.

Solo Flight

With a hint of sadness in his eyes,
He stared past me into the memory of his
　military days
Resurging former urges to scroll the
　warm updrafts,
Meander through flows of
　uncharted fairways
Diving, and rolling to a symphony of
　cosmic delight.
Unfettered from all earthly bonds.

His heart's one desire, alas
Regrettably unresolved these many years,
Remained mingled with yearning
　and regret.
Still, aspiring eyes focused ever upward
Searching the firmament for a reprieve
Throughout his living years.

Anon, the Archangel appeared in a drift
　of roses
Tacitly rejoicing in its mandate
To achieve a quest assigned by
　Divine decree.
Ostensibly squelching all immi-
　nent ambition,
Yet poignantly and fortuitously
Bringing countless penchants to fruition.

Displaying its furtive power and
　mystic might
The good angel of death defies all restric-
　tive ties
That bind Humanity to sorrow, toil, time
　and blight;
Alleviates the agony of suffering, yet
Inadvertently, fulfilling his life-time dream
Fancifully fashioned so long ago.

As the last obstacle benevolently wanes
　in might,
The Teacher ritually snips the shirttails for
　the pilot's quest
Sanctioning approval for his solo flight.
With flight plans duly filed for departure,
An electric sparkle charges the muted
　turbines of the soul.
Behold! He has taken wings! He flies!

Streaming upward in euphoric flight to
　phenomenal heights
Where no mortal being ever strayed,
He blissfully wings his craft towards the
　brilliant light
And the coaxing timbre of the Shepherd's
　beckoning call:
"Come; enter into my Father's house."
Climaxes the awesome experience of his
　earthly life.

Compassion

When offense has been taken
By the crassness of some troll
 Who wounds our fragile spirit
Affecting hatred beyond control.
Bitterness will plague the psychic
Until you vow to take revenge,
Or mutely veer into self-pity
With fists frozen into a clench.
That's when abiding wisdom
Should move us to forgive
The miscreant's ignoble offending act
To live and to let live.
The granting of such mercy
To the one who caused the grief
Takes strength and moral courage
To accord the rogue's relief.
But, our fairness is subverted
When we continually recall the pain
Constantly reliving that single hurt -
A stand that's so inane.

Education – Blood of Life

Higher learning, blood of life,
Fraught with wisdom, just and rife,
Streaming freely down cerebral lanes
To feed the four lobes of the brain.
Expanding exponentially its speed and girth
Augmenting sizably, one's self- worth.

Each coin invested in education,
Improves the process of edification.
Sacrifices that are borne for knowledge,
Are crafted to endure both time and polish;
Provides nourishment for an erudite mind
Unlocking lucrative career finds.

Stifling interest in higher learning
Banishes the chance for greater earning.
Foists a nagging in the heart
To settle for a mediocre part.
Then struggling to make ends meet
Succumbs at end to grim defeat.

Beach Browsing

Children flinging Frisbees betwixt towering pines
Laughing and screaming to their hearts content.
Building sand castles in the sand
With mythical beings girdling their land.

Sailboats charging at angry waves
Spitting sprays of mist onto suntanned skin.
Risky maneuvers bring screams of glee
As skiers challenge the mighty sea.

Dashing and Darting above the lake
Engaged in the sport on water jets.
Sky boarding has hit the modeling stage
As newbies attempt this novel rage.

Campus Hookup

Innocence entered the academia sphere
Seeking knowledge and edification,
Resolved to squelch all impediments
To a well-conceived aspiration

She pours herself a hefty grind
Of labor intense allocations,
Allowing naught for romance
To ruin her lofty ambitions.

Alas, one exhausting evening
Arose an impulse to let go,
After a few tequila shooters
At the campus watering hole.

Quickly her tacit hormones
Respond to this aphrodisiac;
As sensuous urges stir within,
Exposing her bastion to attack

With a brawny male plying her mind,
She seriously starts to bend,
For hooking up was now in vogue -
The current college trends.

Manipulating her sexual charm and wiles
To lure a consenting mate,
Alluring eyes flashed a come-hither look
Undaunted by any consequential fate.

Campus Hookup *(CONTINUED)*

Her carnal leaning was burning strong,
For her mate of sensual needs,
His virility was quick to respond
To her sexy alluring feeds.

Shafts of electrical impulses
Coursed through her pounding brain.
While drifts of promiscuous delight
Drove her utterly insane.

Her buoyant sexuality then consents
To play their loveless game
With reckless abandon for the cost
Of reputation and fame.

In a breathless instant of release,
They break free and depart,
Leaving but a tenuous link
Between their transient hearts.

The coitus usurped the amorous appeal
Of mystique and intrigue
That should exist between newlyweds
In a virginal nuptial league.

Her V-card lost, her innocence gone,
Her dignity sullied hence,
She returns to her academic dorm
Exuding a vacuous stance.

The Great Gift of Time

In the Garden of Eden
From where Adam and Eve proceed,
The concept of time was a foreign entity
Until their expulsion was decreed.

Suddenly, past, present and future
Formed a definable essence
Of uncontrollable and fleeting consciousness
Bearing a stark realistic presence.

Each measurable interval
Utilized throughout each day,
Establishes an unalterable past
Of a legacy, so grandly parlayed!

Actualization of reality emerges
When illness strikes a frightening blow
With a life-threatening prognosis
That shortens life's expected flow.

On bended knee, imploring God
For a miracle to ensue.
He sends His blessed gift of time
Prolonging life for you.

Indignity of Life

When terminal illness finds its victims
In excruciating pain of unbearable size
Patients turn to their practitioner
To effect their own demise.
But laws preclude their assistance
For to legally acquiesce
So, sufferers turn to their own free hand
To alleviate their extreme distress.

As the euthanasia buzz grows louder
Religious groups jump to defend
The sanctity of human life
With petitions that flood the land.
Should their joint efforts succeed
In this most honorable quest,
It will drive the ailing discontents
To seek the second best!

Yet nothing is truly gained
By promulgating this law of the land
But drive the infidel patients
To die by their own sinful hand.
The key to deter these ailing victims
From turning the graveyard sod,
By alleviating the pain they suffer
And put their faith in God.

The Train of Life

The baby's arrival was dramatic
Bouts of crying and kicking were rife
The train was ready for departure
On the erratic journey of life.

As the "All Aboard" command sounded,
The engine began to gather force.
Wheels creaked into action
Along the first leg of the course.

Chugging along the rails of life
To stop at the baptismal font
For a renewal with water
To ease the travelers jaunt.

Continuing the great adventure
To the next leg of the gait,
Stopping just long enough
To be crowned a traveling mate.

At the third stops of the voyage
The train arrives at home.
Scented blossoms adorn the bier
In the chapel beneath the dome.

The journey covered many miles
With sights and sounds unmatched
But, the stops were just a dismal three:
Hatch, match, and dispatch.

Canada's Demise

Simply for want of alteration
Voters demanded political change.
Hell-bent to fix the wheel's rotation
So aptly greased and running free!

The nation made remarkable gains
On the political global stage,
Aiding countries in distress and pains
With financial and combative roles.

Now we've traded our feather bed
For licit murder, drugs and debt.
 A tumor that will quickly spread
As we lapse into a sea of red.

Now we sadly bid a fond adieu
To Canada of our dreams,
Culminating its demise undue
With a requiem service Mass.

A Symbolic Tribute

The medicinal poppy most replete
With euphoric fantasies and boundless peace
Infused with drops of tranquil sleep
Dedicated to Morpheus the God of dreams
Symbolizes fertility and eternal life.

This same poppy of blood red hue
Epitomizes sacrifice for all to view
When fittingly placed near grateful hearts,
Marks our debt to those shining stars.
In remembrance of their sacrifice.

We esteem the price they chose to pay
With crimsoned soil soaked from the fray.
Just ordinary citizens with loyal convictions
Evolved into guardians of our democratic faction,
Giving their all for God and land.

Through noble deeds and highest measure
The reward has been our greatest treasure
Of liberty and freedom for their stand
Through military might, and a divine hand,
We prize these gifts so attained.

 Let moral decay be piously fought,
Lest their sacrifice be for naught!

Helping Hands

They arrive in droves for a short repast
Where open doors convey a friendly home.
 The alluring aroma and a welcome mat
Bring destitute souls to this Heavenly dome.

In a gaunt, and undernourished way,
The growling paunch draws them in
For their only meal, offered each day
Keeping them alive, but frightfully slim.

The endless queue on the well-worn floor
Supports hundreds who wait to appease
The hungry wolf pawing at the door
For a steaming plate of macaroni and cheese.

Charitable people with generous hearts
Offer means to sustain the operation.
Farmers donate surplus yields by carts
To avert these souls from starvation,

When cold winter winds begin to blow
And the temperature drops below
The number of patrons increases in flow
For finding odd jobs tends to slow.

Envision a world with freedom
From poverty, hunger and strife
Where self-sufficiency of families come
As a normality to the comforts of life!

So, Helping Hands reach out to meet
Their physical and spiritual needs.
Providing quality education, replete
Connecting people with solid leads.

Empathy

As we journey on our way
To meet the trials of the day
Perchance a suffering soul will pray
For words of understanding.

Perhaps I too may one day be
Full of care and anxiety.
May those same words return to me
I chose to placate that ailing soul.

In this vast and imperfect world
Many trials are at us hurled
Putting life into a dizzy whirl
Full of unexpected grief.

But, a kind word and a helping hand
Makes life much easier to withstand
When we imitate our Master grand -
Christ our guiding light.

The Incarnation

Behold, this mystically awesome sight
That unfolds for all, this glorious night!
To a lowly manger, in a stable warm,
God appears in humblest form.
From out beneath the swaddling bind,
Extends a hand to humankind.

The Magi's reverence in royal style;
Evokes the child's infectious smile.
His seemingly helpless personality
Will bear the weakness of humanity,
Revealing His unlimited power
With perfection in the weakest hour.

His Projected image, clear and bright
Will transforms darkness into light.
He'll fill our lives with oracles
 And sprinkle earth with miracles.
Such radiant energy of His desire
Will one day set this world afire!

Those in search of truth and Grace
His boundless mercy will embrace.
Noble is His earthly quest,
Promoting life of love and zest.
Resolves to settle our debt one day
Which we incurred but could not pay.

He came to earth as a loving brother
To reconcile us with His Father.
So, honor Him with highest praise
Not just now but all the days.
Greet Him with a welcome hand
To this great impoverished land!

Open House

Doors are open each day at nine.
Come alone or bring some friends.
Plan to stay an hour or more
Discover some new and current trends

Greeters will meet you at the door
With a friendly smile and a welcome hand,
Handing out brochures of layout plans
With room for expansion on demand.

A super salesman will guide you through
The ups and downs of living space.
Note the potential for a carefree home
Prepared for the entire human race.

The Master Carpenter built it well
Gave His all, as He drew the plan
Installed it with a guiding light
To lead us to the promises land.

The Ultimate Sacrifice

Ordained to beautify the dreary land,
The floral bud in crimson train,
In its ardent quest to stay alive
Encounters mounts of rough terrain.

Renowned for innocence and grace,
Though battling pestilence and blight,
Maintains its beauty, rare and pure,
While braving elements day and night.

In due time, the onslaught comes
With pruning shears at lifeline base,
That stems the flow of nutrients
From its blood-red floral face.

The ultimate sacrifice is duly made
Without remorse, yet much at stake.
For time dictates its destiny.
Soon the bloom will fade and flake!

With crimson blood in hand, he pleads
Undying love to his perfect Miss
To appease a lover's inane spat,
Which arose from a neglected kiss.

This ideal symbol of passion and love
Did placate her wounded pride;
For happiness demands a sacrifice.
Forgiveness came, but the rose has died!

The Fickle Wind

This free and playful puff of air
Possesses bursting whimsical fare.
When driven from the frigid north,
Frolics about as a mischievous sort -
Creating cold and brutal storms.

Upon a gleeful and a capricious course
It mocks and teases its counterforce
By pelting snowballs at their bastion
Or flinging ice pellets in merry fashion.
In its familiar disruptive way.

While chasing clouds across the sky
It Spins them round into a high
Creating a tunnel of destructive force
That demolishes structures without remorse
Displaying its cruel abysmal wrath.

It stirs up dust and gives birth
To the dust devils on the earth
Rotating them with frightful speed
To placate its impish need
And sends them screaming heavenward.

Unaccountable for its erratic pleasure
Succumbing only to atmospheric pressure
It recedes into a sense of solemnity
Grudgingly abating its potency
As a scornful pouting child.

In a miraculous change of sudden urges
An utterly new disposition emerges
Wafting a cool and gentle breeze
To relieve and graciously appease
Those bearing the blistering summer heat.

A Farmer's Fate

Such is an agrarian's wisdom:
He knows the time to make hay,
For the weather may impair tomorrow.
So, he works in the sunshine today,

A planter is fully dependent
upon forces beyond one's control.
If there be a harvest to reap,
He must fulfill this incredible role.

Growers grasp the great mystery
Behind the process of planting a crop.
With lack of sufficient sunlight and rain
Germination will slacken and stop.

 A farmer understands his tight schedule;
A phase for work; a spell to wait.
He remains both humble and hopeful
Relying on his knowledge and fate.

Through patience which is his nature,
Blessings are generously bestowed
 Then genuine gratitude ensues within
For a bumper crop, overload!

A Dark Day in September

One sunny Sunday September
After breakfast plates were clear
Mother proposed a short road trip
To visit Gramma dear.
 With joyful glee, the toddlers piled
Into their automobile.
Dad preferred to ride along
So, mother manned the wheel.
Faint thoughts of nervousness
Assailed this chauffeur's candidacy
For she settled into the driver's seat
With a niggling guilt of inadequacy.
 Touring along the busy road
The passengers exploded into song
warbling ditties, they sang in school
In their music sing-a-long.
Soon the crossroad turn appeared
For the northward routed quest

The traffic signal turned to green
Favoring travel east and west.
As the van veered from east to north
A loaded semi came charging west.
The race was on to clear its lane,
Confident she could zip right past.
The sunny Sunday afternoon
Suddenly turned a murky grey
For the semi T-boned the family car
Wiping the entire clan away.
Six lives were lost that sunny day,
Citing Impatience as the cause.
An unwillingness to accept delay
Laid blatant blame for such faux pas.
Midst intolerance and audacity
Dwells this dark personality trait.
The dragon of Impatience chides
When irritated with the wait.

A Nocturnal Visitor

The morn that father was laid to rest
Heavy hearts were borne that day
Lamenting with flooded tears attest
For a vacuous site had claimed its stay.

Emerging from that dreary pit
I could finally lay my head to rest
Conceding a merited respite
From the sorrows that oppressed

While in that sound and restful sleep
A familiar voice beckoned me
That roused me from the calming deep
But not a being could I see.

I felt his presence in my dorm
So near and yet so totally distant.
When I arose the following morn
My gloom had vanished in that instant.

I knew then that in God's hands
Dad was carried off to the promise land
To enjoy the company of family and friends
Where forever collected they would stand.

In God's Hands

I doubt that there will ever be
Life on earth disaster free.
Extreme weather thus assails
With hurricanes and countless gales
Destroying homes and companies
Ruining lives and destinies.
Arid fields caused Kenya's grief
As many plead for food relief.
Entrepreneurs don't seem to care,
Or perhaps they're simply unaware
That polluting the atmosphere
Brings disaster to this hemisphere.
Scientist have cautioned all régimes
To regulate pollutant as most supreme
Yet, capital seems their prime concern
Stoking fossil fuel to burn.
Raging infernos in Canada's west
Displaced so many from their nest.
A massive earthquake struck Mexico
Killing many in its abysmal throw.
This upheaval came on the tail
Of missile testing on a copious scale
Culminating with an exploding bomb
Gifted from Kim Jong Un's palm.
The animal count is in decline
Facing extinction in due time.
The world's in such a disarray
There's nothing left but hope and pray
That all these ills will go away.
And bring back a better day.
Perhaps we're near the end of time
Then this would be my swansong rhyme.

Finding Your True Self

As you listen to the superfluous sounds
Streaming down the auditory canal,
Those peripheral noises that abound
Despoil the spiritual calm.

Wailing sirens screaming, "emergency,"
Automobiles speeding to their destination
Emitting sonorous measures of urgency
Stifle the ability to concentrate.

Planes and trains in discordant harmony
Pollute the space with a de trop din
Cause the brain to slacken and atrophy
And catatonically follow the herd.

Oh, for a clap of thunderous silence
To restore the feeling in the heart and
Promote a deeper sense of ambience
Which defines our inner selves.

To discover that latent identity trait
Necessitates a spell in the wilderness
Away from the distractions and bait
That eschews the noble heart.

Silent solitude admits the heart to convey
Its true feeling to the receptive mind.
Then you will readily discover and say
This is who I really am!

Children at Play

On the first day of kindergarten school
Two boys were challenged with a duel.
Donald and Kim were given some clay
To mold a beautiful world one day.

Kim's stature was dismally small
Donald's figure was relatively tall.
But both their ego's one could say
Were as large as a stack of hay.

Soon their project work began
As they laid out their global plan.
Donald kept an eagle eye on Kim
And would not be upstaged by him.

Then Donald began to note
That Kim was trying to get his goat
By firing rockets into the air.
This gave Donald a bit of a scare.

In return Donald vowed to stoop
And obliterate the little droop.
But, name calling instead took affect
As they fought for mutual respect

Little Rocket man was Kim's new name
Dotard was Donald's claim to fame.
Eventually name calling progressed
And a declaration of war was expressed.

The threats were frequent and many
Yet, such action was devoid of any.
That is the present state this day
Of two kindergartens kids at play.

The Tree of Life

There never was a tree so grand
A tree that means so much to me
As one that formed that hideous stand
On which there hung an innocent man
Who suffered there in great torment;
A faultless victim of a hateful plan.

Of His own accord He chose this path
To redeem us from infernal strife.
Devoid of jealousy, hate and wrath,
He paved the road to eternity
Through compassion and self-sacrifice
With abiding love for humanity.

That humble tree while once unknown
Delightfully played its part that day,
For it gave the Savion on its own
His choice to save all humankind;
Thereby reconciling us with His Father
To live our lives with peace of mind.

Oh, tree of life, you came to be
An instrument of redeeming grace.
With grateful hearts we all agree
Your contribution to His cause
Was paramount to God's plan.
So, for your aid, give our applause!

Sonnets

A Seasoned Love

We made the choice our love to share
Those many fleeting years gone by.
On altar vows we relied
To bind our nuptial life with care.
With bands of gold to attest and bare,
This symbol of our vows we plied,
A penchant for deceit belie,
On Satan's guiles, we must beware.

Our love has grown with leaps and bounds;
More opulent than Maharajas' gems,
Keener than the scent of hounds,
Deeper than the mighty Thames.
Genuine love knows no bounds
Akin the bards' romantic poems.

The Living Light

The stellar orbs that bedeck the nebulous cosmos
And diminish the darkness by their radiant essence,
Were deliberately fashioned for an ephemeral existence,
To expire when they have served their designed purpose;
With a violent explosion at the end of their useful phase,
The remnant debris plummets expeditiously to the ground,
And finds its niche beneath an earthly mound
Henceforth consigned to its eternal resting place.

Reflective of these stars are we that inhabit this earth
With perishable bodies largely composed of stardust;
are likewise created to tentatively fulfill the creator's quest
'Till death explosively extinguishes the living light of birth
And lodges the remains beneath the earthly crust.
But the righteous soul attains an eternally spiritual fest.

The Ills of the land

Despite adversities that befall this mortal life,
Political blunders arise to ruin a pristine land,
Factory pollutants add fodder to the strife
Until death is poised to rap a crushing hand!

What will redeem us and lend support,
To propagate an environmental diffusion?
Indifference will not rectify this ugly sort,
Merely function as a liquor of self-delusion.

Whom shall we go to with our urgent appeal
To forcibly eradicate this formidable foe?
When will we bring the world back to ideal
And cleanse the earth of this terrible woe?

The key to this dilemma is quite unclear
But, a leap of Faith will mitigate the fear.

The Frugal Angler

He purchased a fish-finder for the quest
Stashed hooks and rods in his pickup truck.
Towed the boat to a lake assessed,
Then, beseeched the Lord to grant him luck

Deeming every trout, he'd lure the while,
Would fetch a saving of plenteous pence.
While posturing mastery over nature's guiles -
A worthy token of recompense.

Idly trawling the lake all day
Ne'er a nibble did come to be.
Precious hours he whiled away
Were gone forever, lost at sea!

His one response to this vagary dream -
"Ah, but the meditation was supreme!"

Nature's Blush

Beach blankets dotted the manicured lawn
Staked by young adults in semi-clad dress.
Their tanning bods glistening in the midday sun
Soaking up wellness for the winter stress.

Portable chairs strewn about shady sites
For modest seniors to bridge the day.
Sitting prim and proper in their lily whites
Savoring novels laced with racy exposé.

Seagulls diving for abandoned ort
At emptied basket on the greens.
Then dropping bombs on unsuspecting sort
As they mirthfully flee the picnic scenes.

I sat and spied Mother Nature blush
As she coyly dealt me this royal flush!

Romantic Love

How uplifting and abysmal the passion
Which elicits a pleasurable feeling
For another human being
When expressed in reciprocal fashion.
A touch of the hand, a cheerful smile
Propels the relationship along
Arousing love ballads in song
With gifted red roses for style.

This evolution of romantic love
Which may span from months to a year
Forms an enduring durable link.
Mutating to grace from above
It brings the joyful couple near
The nectar of connubial drink.

A Tragic Finale

Many years were cherished together
By the loving couple once they wed.
They conquered hurdles, and boldly tread
Through wild and stormy weather.
Their children count was twelve in number
But, with Christian love and duties' call
Together they raised them one and all
With ne'er a moan to encumber.

As the years kept slipping by
A tragic illness claimed his wife,
Which extinguished their wedded bliss.
Despondence shackled his dismal try
To regain composure of his life;
But despair crafted him a bleak abyss.

Great Achievement Race

From the very early years of life
Our focus has been on possession
So, accumulations were rife
With toys of every expression.
The earthly crown was enticing
As we sped down the road of success.
Accumulating wealth was exciting
Despite the curse of duress.
The social ladder was extremely steep
To achieved upward mobility.
So, morals and virtues were laid to sleep
To achieve superiority.
    Pride, arrogance and envy reigned supreme
    As we chased that elusive dream

The Changing World

Although citizens are unconfined to cages
The depressed can feel the devastation
As downsizing and restructuring rages
To stave off company liquidation.
Consumers who shop on line
Put local businesses in a squeeze,
Causing their employees to find
Work with other companies.
With a lack of marketable skills
For alternative reemployment
The applicant's progress stills
With rejection and disappointment.
    It's time to join the local band:
    Support the commerce of our land

Where Lies the Blame?

Covetousness, Avarice, and Greed,
Such are the troubles and frets
Befalling our society indeed
Through overextended household debts.
From soaring food and utilities prices,
A perfect economic storm unfurled
Birthing fraudster's, and scammer's vices
Permeating our technology world.
Those obsessively devoted for more stash
Fall prey to the chicanery of vultures
That bilk victims of their hard-earned cash.
Creating an idiosyncratic culture.
    Ironically the Scammers' dupes
    Fall prey to their own greedy bloops.

The Frightful "C" Word

For decades, cancer has claimed many lives
Compelling a frantic search for a cure.
Thus, many victims were moved to procure
Financial assistance from charity drives.
Recent years have elicited high-fives
 When it was established for sure
That half of the cases have a preventable cure
By thus embarking on healthy life-style strives.

Consume a whole-food diet without additives,
Remain active and control your weight,
Add half an aspirin to your daily regimen imperatives
And avoid undue stress in your mandate.
If you eschew all these causal allurements
You are lowering the cancer rate.

Prose

The Changing Seasons

The chilly autumn winds gust in
With tints of beauty to the realm
in a kaleidoscope of dazzling blushes.
Soon every stem in the field,
And all the foliage from the trees,
Is strewed about the entire spread;
Laid to bed by the killing frost.

As bitter winter closes in,
gleaming in its pure majestic robe,
it conceals the ugliness left behind
By autumn's callous slovenliness.
An ideal time to be at home
In cozy comfort of a couch,
Resting warmly by the hearth.

Spring hustles in with a cleansing rain
To swab away autumn's shriveled leaves
Exposed by the melting snow.
Soon the fields are clothed with grass,
Every bud bursts forth with foliage green;
Plants erupt into gorgeous blooms,
And the land reclaims its rich attire.

Summer sidles in as a cherished friend.
Time for travel on a well-earned break.
A slowing down of the pulse of days,
Evenings long, mornings bright,
Summer breezes cool and light.
Steaks a sizzling on the open grill
Comfort living, a time to chill.

These four seasons summarize
The totality of our earthly lives;
Spring, symbolic of our birth;
Summer, evolving and living large;
Autumn, prosperity and returns,
Winter, peace and solace earned
In a tranquil Heavenly home.

Prisoner of the Mind

Fear, doubt and confusion,
Are a terrible troubling trio
Possess enough power
to paralyze the human mind.
This brood of fearmongers
Have resolved in their dire quest
To create and sustain forever
Inexorable prison walls.
To flee this dungeon of the mind
Commands a ritual and common code:
Concentrate only on the task ahead
Deemed mandatory to achieve.
Listen to your inner voice of amity
Calling out to fulfil your charge.
Move outside your comfort zone
And obey the higher calling
Of cordial love and devotion.
The prison door will unlock!
As you exit, realize
The love you possess
Will always set you free
To pursue your future with alacrity.

Consequences

I casually tossed a pebble, oh so small
into a shallow lake nearby.
So, what? Who cares?
Ripples formed on glassy skin.
The nugget sank into the deep
For a long and soggy sleep.
A passing minnow deemed it food
Then spit it out; it was no good!
A disappointing find for a hungry fish!

I innocently tossed a hefty rock
onto a vacant neighbor's lot.
So, what? Who cares?
It hit the ground with an awful thud.
A crawling ant happened by that way
Gathering food for its hungry brood.
Forgetting to duck, it caught the rock
Unexpectedly by surprise
And caused the ant's demise.
The family's now in disarray
Without a hunter or a prey.

I naively nudged a boulder, huge
To tumble down a county hill.
So, what? Who cares?
It crushed some daisies in its path,
And sealed the port of a gopher hole.
Barreling across a busy road
It gouged a mark on a passing rig
Causing it to swerve and roll;
Unable to complete its intended trip.
The motorist was badly scratched,
So, an ambulance was dispatched.
Rushing to aid the man in pain,
It accidently slammed into a train.
Both driver and patient once full of life
On that tragic day did not survive.

Every action, be it large or small
bears consequences that befall.
Problems arise when unthinkingly
We ignore to ponder willingly
On the consequences of our deeds
That appease our impulsive needs.

My Conscience, My Friend

Somewhere in the recesses of my heart
Dwells a childhood friend and kindred spirit
Endowed with tenacity, yet compassion.
A pal who eagerly shares my discomforts,
and ameliorates my frequent hurts,
Or basks in the glory of my successes!
A confidant so resilient and caring
Who, while gladly bearing my foibles
Gently guides me through myriads of protocols,
Unimpeded by my countless episodes
 of feebleness and vacillations.
An entity that transforms and shapes
my weak resolve into tempered steel
To withstand all life's travails and falls
That will surely reoccur.
A pal that knows no bounds,
Listens to my every word and sound,
Agrees with all I do and say,
Not judgmental in any way.
These are the qualities of a true friend;
Always faithful to the end.

The Joy of Aging

Through youthful years I admired
The wisdom of dear old dad;
A caring soul for his progeny,
Who handled life with greatest ease.
I prized the fortitude of mother's drive
Who carried troubles without fear.
Presuming age begets wisdom,
A longing for the golden years
Ached within my young heart.
In dismay, as years rolled by
Aging began to take its toll.
Father Time, in beard and robe
wielding his sickle erratically,
Morphed into a crass beautician
Carving deep wrinkles in the brow;
Turning hair, a dreary gray.
Then came the failings to embrace:
Teeth extractions, hearing aids,
Senior moments, vision loss,
Creaking bones, aching joints,
Precarious balance and co-ordination,
Atrophied muscles from lack of use.
The beating heart revved up its drive
Struggling to pump the blood of life
Through conduits of stiffened pipes
Clogged with plaque from affluence.
Sadly, wisdom did not come with age,
Golden years arrived but not the sage.

Haiku

Plying autumn mist
Master painter's skilled hands
Veils his masterpiece.

Skeletal bones mourn
O'er unsightly charred remains
Of a better day

Luscious cranberries
Enhance a turkey dinner
Fodder for the bears

Pleasing waves of life
Wash ashore spritely starfish
To untimely death

Cold frosty snowflakes
Clothe nature's vegetation
In comforting warmth.

Nature's living shade
Crafted symmetrically
Wrecked by autumn frost

Mature autumn leaves
Abandon comforts of home
For rank compost bins.

Frozen cranberries
Fermenting on leafless vines
Buzz party waxwings.

Dark menacing clouds
Hover over tranquil bay
Illuminating the calm.

Clichéd Golden Years
Attained by aging couples
Bring forth loneliness

The energetic young
Thinking themselves infallible
End up in the grave

Compassionate ones
Who have suffered extremely
Take aging in stride.

Seekers of pleasure
Who resort to opioids
Woo untimely death.

The hard knocks in life
Carve deep furrows on the face;
A badge of valor.

Arrogance and pride
Uplift the bruising ego
To isolation.

Thunder and lightning
Forecasted a huge downpour
That modestly fared!

Edward Cornwallis
Founded Halifax city.
Tribute veiled by tarp.

Young Omar Kadar
Performed a terrorist act
Rewarded by cash.

Limericks

There was a young man of class
Whose lovemaking was terribly crass.
The surgeon's sharp knife
Changed his whole life
By turning him into a lass.

A youth who came from Sudan
Devised a terrorist plan.
He designed an explosive
With a dastardly motive
Then let it explode in his hand

A Sculptor in Fine Arts class
Just loved to tease and harass.
His peers had enough
Of his annoying stuff
And polished his sorry brass.

One day a rummy, half lit
Stumbled and fell into a pit.
When he finally arose
He was holding his nose
For he was totally covered with grit.

A gay who lacked a mate
Asked a lesbian out on a date.
They spent the whole night
Discussing their plight.
By morning both shifted to straight.

While alone in the house one day
A tiny mouse happened to stray.
With a quick of the mind
She flashed her behind,
And blew the varmint away.

There was a man from Calais
Who picked up a call girl one day.
When asked, "What's your pleasure?"
He replied in full measure,
"Iron my clothes, today!"

Wherever you happen to be
Let your wind always go free
For withholding inside
May heighten your pride
But bloated and miserable you'll be.

A lady from the Isle of Man
Had wrapped herself up in Saran
Her husband was floored
When she opened the door
And quipped, "What? Left overs again, Fran!"

There once was a man named Bond
Of martinis, he was notably fond
One day he concocted a mix
Truly a connoisseur's fix
That got all the ladies bombed

There was a redneck named Jed
Who slept on a feathery bed
When it came to wash sheets
He used the vacuum of Pete's
Leaving but a vacuous spread.

There was a lady from Cowan
Who always was seen with a frown.
She was unwed
For she couldn't bake bread
But her parakeets were the nicest in town

A young maiden who lived in Mundare
Simply refused to shorten her hair.
She grew it quite long
Down to her knees it was hung
Now, on her horse she could ride bare.

A kid who pulled a dumb prank
Lobbed a live grenade at a Yank.
In Gitmo, he served time
Until released for his crime
With fifteen million clams to bank.

A man from the north they say
Was playing with his rocket one day.
He let it fly high
To see where it would fly
As the world ducked for cover to pray.

Index

Mike Henry TKACHUK

I was born and raised in a small village of Angusville, in Manitoba, Canada. Upon completion of high school at Major Pratt Collegiate in Russell, Manitoba, I attended the Universities of Manitoba, Brandon University, and Ottawa University; the recipient of these degrees: B.A., B.Ed., M.Ed., and a certificate in Eastern Christian Studies. I hold an Education Administrator's Level II certificate, and a province of Manitoba Teaching Certificate. After serving in the Canadian Armed Forces for four years both in Canada and abroad, with the Royal Canadian Army Medical Corps, I was employed as a teacher/ principal in the elementary and junior High grades. After graduating from the Catholic Seminary in Ottawa, I am employed as pastor of St. Mary's Ukrainian Catholic Churches in Brandon and Portage la Prairie, Manitoba. I am married to my wife Dolores. My first poetry book, "Poetry, My Obsession", was published in 2011.